Habitat Selection and Changes in the White-tailed and Black-tailed

PRAIRIE DOG

Population

within the Northern Bighorn Basin, Wyoming

Technical Note 431
September 2009

White-tailed prairie dog

By:

Destin Harrell
Wildlife Biologist
Bureau of Land Management
Cody Field Office, Wyoming

Lisa Marks
Geologist
Bureau of Land Management
Cody Field Office, Wyoming

Black-tailed prairie dog, Randy Hayes, BLM

ACKNOWLEDGMENTS

WE WOULD LIKE TO THANK Joe Capodice, retired biologist for the BLM. He helped inspire our prairie dog survey. Steve Kiracofe was a big help for the soil survey analysis as was Richard Lowry with statistical questions. Field crew members who were kind enough to collect much of the data for this publication include Brian Latta, Bill Palmeroy, Katie VinZant, and Darci Stafford. Dean Biggins, Dennis Saville, Bob Oakleaf, and Martin Grenier offered much helpful advice and review. Bill Wilson was always there for GPS and GIS data processing. Mike Stewart was generous in offering reviews, ideas, and support. Kathy Rohling and Janine Koselak at the National Operations Center contributed invaluable efforts by editing, arranging, and drawing original artwork for this paper. And finally, thanks to the Bureau of Land Management's Cody Field Office staff and management for helping with this collaborative effort.

Burrowing owls

CONTENTS

ABSTRACT vii

INTRODUCTION 1

STUDY AREA 3

METHODS 5

RESULTS 7
    Population Demographics 7
    Habitat Associations 9

DISCUSSION 11

LITERATURE CITED 15

Burrowing owls, a prairie dog associate, frequently nest in empty burrows.

White-tailed prairie dog

ABSTRACT

WITHIN THE NORTHERN BIGHORN BASIN, Wyoming, prairie dog *(Cynomys)* survey data collected between 1980 and 1989 were compared with data from a 2001–2005 survey. From these data, distribution, activity level, and habitat selection based on range site and precipitation categories were analyzed. Overall, the white-tailed prairie dog *(C. leucurus)* population declined in distribution and activity. Occupied active area decreased 71 percent from 7,031.8 ha (17,374.9 ac) to 2,011.5 ha (4,970.6 ac); there was also a 37 percent decrease in active town abundance and a 55 percent

decrease in the mean active town area. Declines in occupied area for the Meeteetse Metapopulation (87 percent) were greater than declines for the remaining population (Basin Metapopulation - 39 percent). There was also a very small population of black-tailed prairie dogs *(C. ludovicianus)* that increased 8 percent to 77.4 ha (191.3 ac). Density of active burrows declined significantly (P < 0.006) for the Basin Metapopulation. The mean nearest neighbor distances separating white-tailed prairie dog towns for both surveys were

approximately 2.0 km. Towns appear to be significantly associated with saline upland, loamy, sandy, shallow loamy, and shale range sites (P < 0.0001). White-tailed prairie dogs were also significantly associated with precipitation zones (P < 0.0001) and may prefer the 20.3–25.4 cm (8–10 in) precipitation zone even though they were more common in the 12.7–22.9 cm (5–9 in) precipitation zone. Other variables not measured also likely contribute to the observed distribution of white-tailed prairie dog town site selection.

Landscape of the Meeteetse prairie dog metapopulation

Mountain plover, endemic to North America, find prairie dog towns to be good nesting habitat.

INTRODUCTION

PRAIRIE DOGS *(Cynomys spp.)*, are often described as a keystone species and ecological engineers (Miller et al. 1994; Bangert and Slobodchikoff 2000), have declined as much as 98 percent throughout North America since European settlement (Ceballos and Reading 1994). Viability of several species has become an important biodiversity issue. All species are listed or have been petitioned for listing under the Endangered Species Act of 1973.

This biodiversity issue is relevant in the Bighorn Basin, Wyoming, where white-tailed prairie dogs *(C. leucurus)* are near the northern extent of their range and where four black-tailed prairie dog *(C. ludovicianus)* towns are grouped together near the city of Cody, Wyoming (Seglund et al. 2004). The origin of these sympatric black-tailed prairie dogs, isolated within the white-tailed

prairie dog range is unknown. Speculation includes release from captivity or an isolated population of their former range.

White-tailed prairie dogs and black-tailed prairie dogs have different life histories and may influence the ecosystem in different ways. White-tailed prairie dogs may clip vegetation less than black-tailed prairie dogs (Clark 1973). During the winter, white-tailed prairie dogs may enter torpor at an ambient air temperature of 7° C for longer periods of time than black-tailed prairie dogs, which are facultative hibernators during winter (Harlow and Menkens 1986; Lehmer and Biggins 2005). Both species alter their environment, providing unique habitat for associated species, and can be a substantial prey base for predators (Campbell and Clark 1981; Knowles et al. 1982; Miller et al. 1994; Weltzin et al. 1997).

The black-footed ferret *(Mustela nigripes)* preys upon prairie dogs for the majority of its diet and is one of many species associated with and adapted to prairie dog towns (Hillman et al. 1979; Campbell and Clark 1981; Cambell et al. 1987). During the evening of September 26, 1981, a black-footed ferret was killed by a rancher's dog approximately 48 km (30 miles) south of Cody and a few kilometers west of Meeteetse, Wyoming; the consequential live capture of the once thought extinct black-footed ferret occurred in October 1981 (Menkens and Anderson 1991). In 1985, sylvatic plague *(Yersinia pestis)* was discovered in the prairie dog metapopulation near Meeteetse where the population of black-footed ferrets was discovered (Menkens and Anderson 1991).

These discoveries helped to prompt James Bredy and Steven Coy of the Bureau of Land

Management's (BLM) Cody Resource Area to begin surveys for prairie dogs. Surveys were conducted between 1980 and 1989 using a variety of techniques for locating and mapping white-tailed prairie dog colonies including, but not limited to, infrared aerial photography, helicopter flights, personal communications, and ground observations. These data were used to inventory prairie dog towns, better identify potential habitat for black-footed ferrets, and to produce a Prairie Dog Ecosystem Habitat Management Plan (Coy and Roberts 1985). Their study area excluded the Meeteetse Metapopulation, which was mapped independently by the U.S. Fish and Wildlife Service (FWS) on 1:100,000 maps in 1988 (Coy and Roberts 1985).

This report compares data from the survey conducted by the BLM in 2001–2005 with the 1980–1989 surveys conducted by the BLM and FWS, and summarizes changes in indices of distribution and abundance. The 2001–2005 data were also used for analysis of habitat associations. Methods were used similar to those in 1980–1989, which made comparisons possible with acknowledgement of biases, limitations, and errors when replicating historical surveys. These data may help identify trends in populations; however, these trends do not identify the many factors that may affect prairie dog distribution and abundance.

Prairie dog distribution and activity may be regulated by their natural history, which is different for white-tailed and black-tailed prairie dogs (Hoogland 1996). Prairie dog towns are not randomly distributed and towns may be clumped (Hillman et al. 1979). Prairie dogs produce one litter per year with an average of 3.08 to 3.88 pups, and survival may be less than 60 percent in the first year (Clark and Stromberg 1987; Hoogland 2001). Female harassment may

be caused by a shortage of unrelated females in the coterie, encouraging dispersal (Garrett and Franklin 1988). In Albany County, Wyoming, pups began to disperse at the time when the population density was greatest (late June and early July) (Clark 1973). Young, dispersing males tended to occupy old, uninhabited burrow systems (Clark 1973). Some adults may also emigrate, leaving the young behind, possibly due to the animosity of other adults (Koford 1958).

Immigration and emigration factors appear to be related to prairie dog population fluctuations (Tileston and Lechleitner 1966). There have been few studies on dispersal and reported distances are usually maximum observations. Garrett and Franklin (1988) report an average black-tailed prairie dog dispersal distance of 2.4 km, but Koford (1958) observed black-tailed prairie dogs emigrating nearly 6.5 km. Clark (1973) recorded white-tailed prairie dogs moving 2.7 km during emigration between March and April and between July and August. Hillman et al. (1979) reported that the mean distance between black-tailed prairie dog towns and their nearest neighbors was 2.4 km. As prairie dogs emigrate and establish new towns, they select habitat based on criteria that have not been fully defined. If habitat selection criteria were better defined, then efforts to conserve potential habitat might be more successful.

Habitat selection can vary greatly and might be explained by many factors, including environmental conditions, vegetation barriers, and prairie dog control efforts (Cambell III and Clark 1981; Coppock and Detling 1986; Weltzin et al. 1997). Data indicating prairie dog selection of certain soil and precipitation characteristics appears to be limited and information for the Bighorn Basin is needed. Other studies have observed new

burrows in soils that are dense clay-clayey-saline uplands correlated with the cessation of annual plant growth or existing growth dehydration (Clark 1973; Parker et al. 1975).

The vegetative community and structure can also influence the distribution of prairie dogs (Osborn and Allan 1949; Weltzin et al. 1997). Prairie dogs feed mainly on annual forbs and other plants typical of early successional stages, and their herbivory can increase shoot nitrogen concentrations (Bond 1945; Holland and Detling 1990). Their food habits vary with the time of year and the availability of vegetation (Tileston and Lechleitner 1966). Generally, black-tailed prairie dogs may eat mostly forbs and grasses, while the white-tailed prairie dogs may eat more grasses and sedges (Tileston and Lechleitner 1966). Prairie dog movement can be restricted in some cases by tall vegetation such as greasewood; however, white-tailed prairie dogs are more tolerant of taller vegetation than black-tailed (Clark 1973; Hoogland 1996; Weltzin et al. 1997). Absence of prairie dogs can increase woody vegetation seed dispersal and alter species composition (Osborn and Allan 1949; Weltzin et al. 1997). Rosenstock and Van Riper III (2001) report active prairie dog towns were present in grasslands uninvaded by shrubs and absent in successional woodlands, indicating aversion to woody vegetation encroachment.

Prairie dog distribution and activity are dependent on many known and unknown biotic and abiotic attributes. The study area was defined and inventory methods were used in 2001–2005 that were similar to methods for the 1980–1989 BLM survey. This report describes trends in course scale population indices spanning 12 to 26 years, and also analyzes soil type and precipitation zone selection for the prairie dog population.

Habitat Selection and Change in the White-tailed and Black-tailed Prairie Dog Populations within the Northern Bighorn Basin, Wyoming

White-tailed prairie dog

STUDY AREA

THE PRAIRIE DOG TOWNS within the study area (Total Population) were divided into two metapopulations: the Basin Metapopulation and the Meeteetse Metapopulation. The Basin Metapopulation area was south of the Montana and Wyoming State line, east of the Shoshone National Forest, west of the Bighorn National Forest, and north of Shell Creek and the Greybull River (Figure 1). The Meeteetse Metapopulation area was defined as towns west of Highway 120, north of the Greybull River and the Wood River, east of the Shoshone National Forest and south of Latitude 44° 19′ 40.00″ North (Figure 1). An observed white-tailed prairie dog dispersal distance of 2.7 km (Clark 1973) was used to separate the Meeteetse Metapopulation from the Basin Metapopulation.

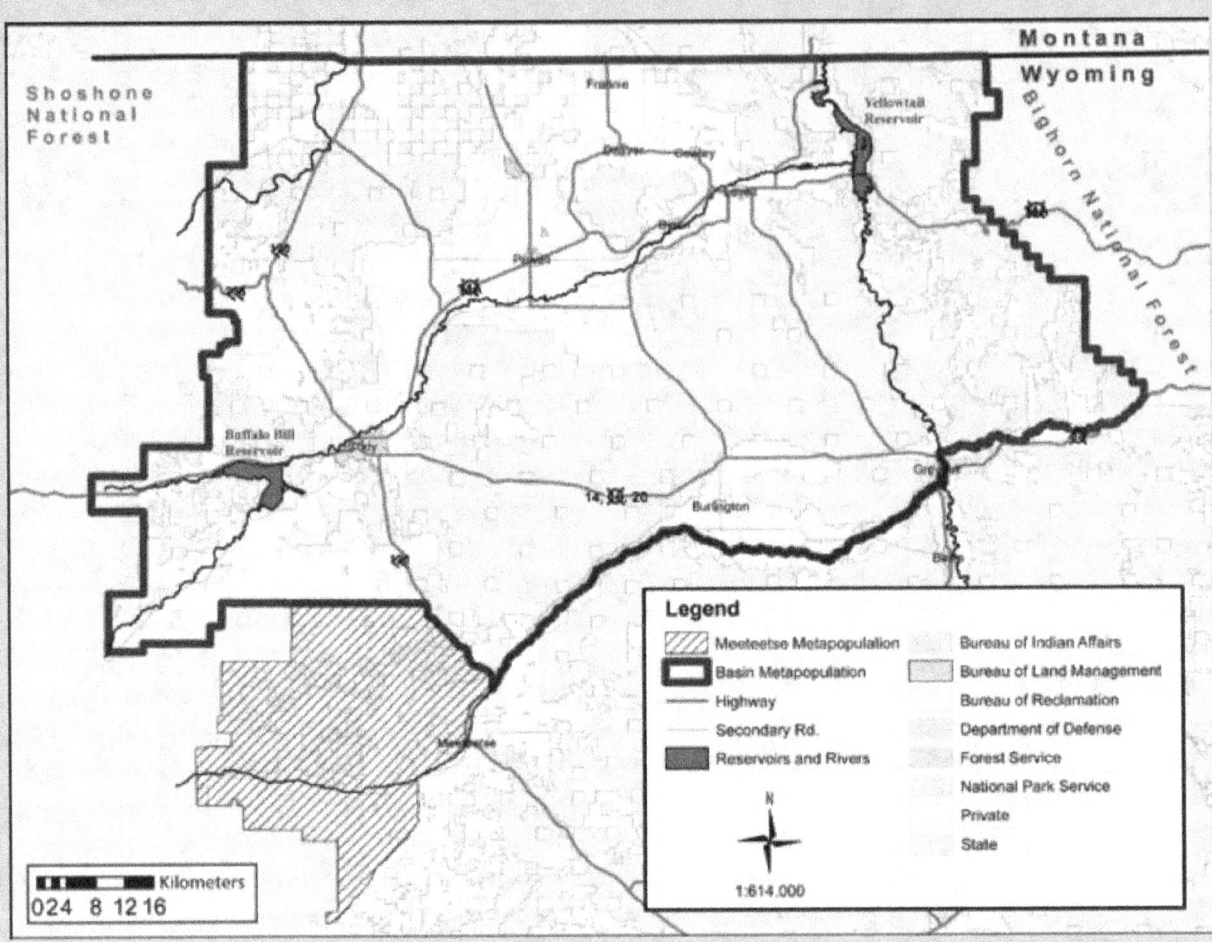

Figure 1. The study area includes the Total Population, which is equal to the Basin Metapopulation plus the Meeteetse Metapopulation survey areas.

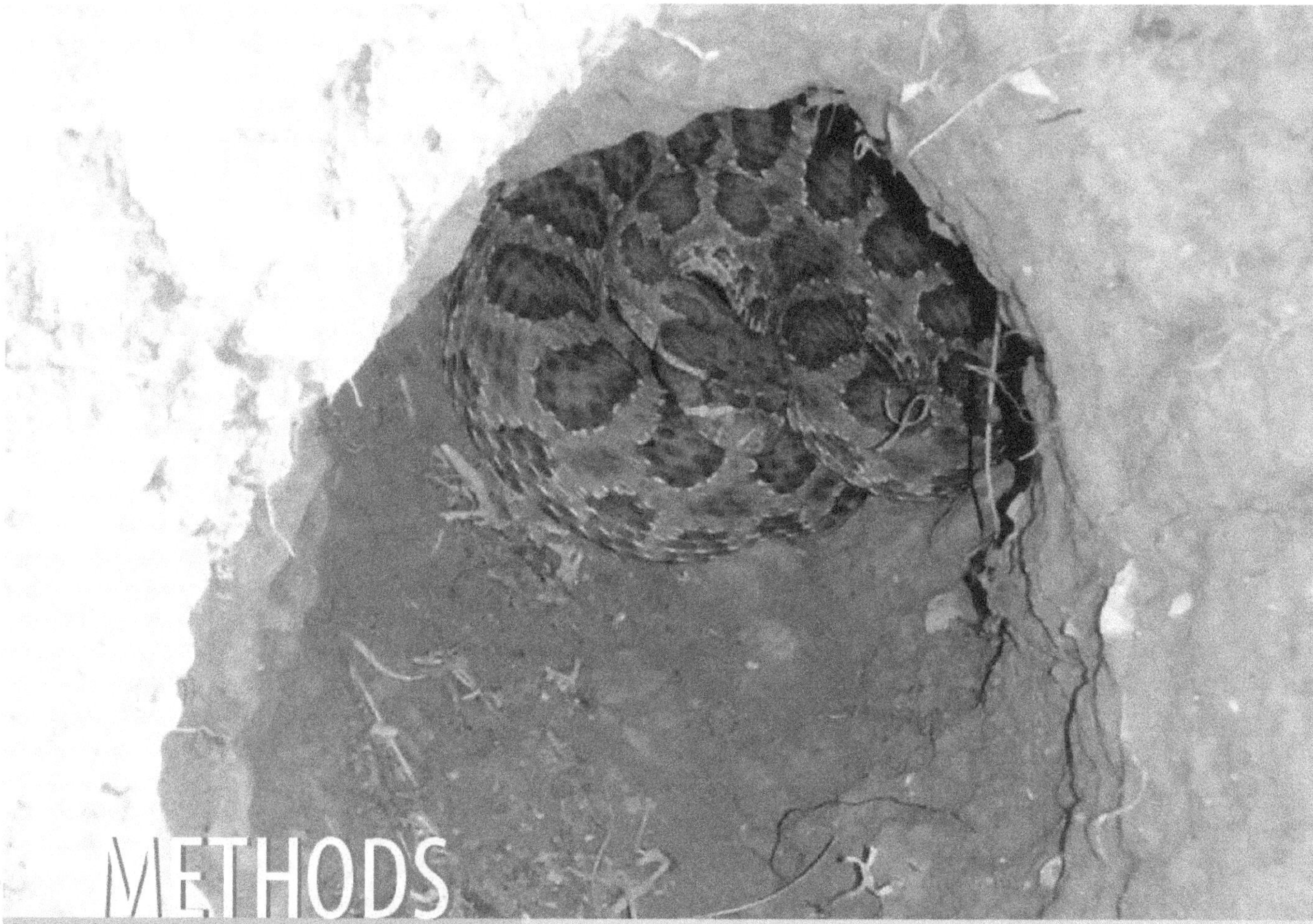

Prairie rattlesnake occupying a black-tailed prairie dog burrow.

METHODS

THE 1980–1989 SURVEY was identified as including two major survey efforts, the 1980–1989 BLM survey data and the Meeteetse Metapopulation survey (mapped by the FWS on 1:100:000 mylar in 1988), which together surveyed the study area with similar land access issues and did not include lands up the South Fork of the Shoshone River. Active prairie dog town locations from these maps were screen digitized and areas were calculated in GIS Arc Map 9.1 ESRI 2005. Active 1980–1989 towns were assigned a new consecutive town "ID" number by sorting through unknown and inactive towns. These numbers were linked to the original survey numbers, referenced in GIS and on data sheets in a new Prairie Dog Survey Binder and added to a database in Microsoft Office Access 2003. These data were then compared to a new survey conducted by the BLM between 2001 and 2005.

Because it took multiple years to accumulate data, the surveys are not instantaneous descriptions. Results represented active prairie dog towns found during the surveys, but surveys may not have been complete. The FWS survey did not include the same methods used by the 1980–1989 BLM survey; therefore, town burrow activity levels in the Meeteetse Metapopulation were not analyzed or compared to the 2001–2005 survey.

In an effort to replicate the former survey with similar methods, surveys were conducted from April through November. Surveys were conducted on BLM, Bureau of Reclamation (BOR), state, and private lands when access was granted in potential prairie dog habitat, which included vegetation communities that were not in river bottoms, irrigated fields, forests, alpine, and subalpine areas. All previously

identified prairie dog towns were resurveyed. Aerial photography and former survey results assisted in locating prairie dog towns. In addition to ground observations, local residents were interviewed to increase detection rates. Ridges and roads were driven or walked to maximize the visual area surveyed. The most effective method for finding prairie dog towns appeared to be binocular searches from elevated locations (Coy and Roberts 1985). Aircraft surveys are effective but were precluded due to expense. Once a town was identified, its location was recorded as a polygon using a global positioning system (Trimble GeoExplorer 3).

Town boundaries were defined by walking the perimeter to the closest burrow or mound, recording data with a GPS unit. A town was considered new if its boundaries did not overlap a town identified during a previous survey. Once every data collection season on relatively high, medium, and low density towns, a measuring wheel was used to conduct 1 meter wide transects oriented north and south distributed every 30 m parallel to each other continuing to the edges of the town to calibrate observer estimates for burrow density (Biggins et al. 1993). For the study, active and inactive burrow densities were estimated and placed within categories of ≤10 or >10 burrows per 0.405 ha (1.0 ac). A Prairie Dog Town Inventory Form was filled out according to the Cody Resource Area Prairie Dog Ecosystem Habitat Management Plan (Coy and Roberts 1985); the town was then assigned an identification number and incorporated into the database.

Data were analyzed for active towns within the Total Population and analyzed separately as the Meeteetse Metapopulation and the Basin Metapopulation (Figure 1). Any number of active burrows mapped at the finest resolution was considered a "town." A town was considered active if there were any recent prairie dog signs of activity such as: observed individuals, fresh scat, vocalizations, and fresh excavation (Biggins et al. 2006). Data for inactive towns were not collected or analyzed during this survey; however, inactive burrows within an active town were used to estimate the inactive burrow density. Inactive prairie dog towns are present throughout the landscape, and they may be recently inactive or may have been inactive for many years (Biggins et al. 2006). Although inactive towns are very important to wildlife still occupying the area, it could not be determined how long a town had been inactive and so they were not collected since they would not

indicate current prairie dog distribution or abundance.

Nearest town distances for all 2001–2005 white-tailed prairie dog towns were measured using GIS ArcMap 9.1 ESRI 2005. Summary statistics were produced for measured distances from the outer edge boundaries of all white-tailed prairie dog towns to the next nearest town edge. Nearest distances were averaged to produce the mean distance to the nearest neighboring town.

Soil type and precipitation zone selection analysis were based on "Actual" and "Potential" use. The 2001–2005 active white-tailed prairie dog town areas were analyzed as Actual use areas. A 2.7 km buffer area around the Actual use areas were analyzed as Potential use areas for white-tailed prairie dogs and it was assumed this buffer incorporated potential habitat for selection based on dispersal observations (Clark 1973).

In GIS, Actual and Potential areas were overlaid on top of Park and Bighorn County's soil surveys, which also included precipitation zone data that are digitized, initial field work performed by the BLM and the Soil Conservation Service, now the Natural Resources Conservation Service (NRCS), in the late 1970s and early 1980s. Total soil type areas and precipitation areas were calculated within the Actual and Potential areas.

The resulting soil type areas were divided into range site areas using the percent occurrence listed in the map unit. For instance, a town was found to have

247.1 ha (610.0 ac) of soil type 474AD, which generally has range sites with 40 percent shale, 50 percent saline upland, and 10 percent that is "not specified." Therefore, the area was proportioned by percentage and it was assumed that 98.7 ha (244.0 ac) were used in shale sites, 123.4 ha (305.0 ac) were in saline uplands, and 24.7 ha (61.0 ac) were not named. Unspecified soil types were excluded from the analysis.

Area and percent occurrence of each precipitation zone were also calculated. Using the five most frequent range sites and the three precipitation zones, which overlap [12.7–22.9 cm (5–9 in), 20.3–25.4 cm (8–10 in), and 25.4–35.6 cm (10–14 in)]; a two-dimensional chi square test was performed between the Actual and the Potential available area (2.7 km buffer). This method assumes all range sites within a soil type are used equivalently as often as they occur and that soil surveys for private lands were not entirely complete.

Descriptive data analyses were primarily conducted in Microsoft Office Excel 2003. A two-dimensional chi-square test was used to test for significant associations between the two surveys and the two categories of burrow density, the two categories of activity level, precipitation zone area, and range site area within 2.7 km of the white-tailed prairie dog town edge and the area within towns. The Frequency unit was per hectare for the precipitation and range site statistical analysis. Null hypotheses were rejected at $\alpha = 0.05$. Statistical tests were performed in Microsoft Excel 2003 and in VassarStats: Web Site for Statistical Computation (Lowry 2007).

White-tailed prairie dog

RESULTS

Population Demographics

The 1980–1989 survey results for the Total Population:

There were 105 active white-tailed towns occupying 7,031.8 ha (17,374.9 ac) with a minimum area of 0.008 ha (0.02 ac) and a maximum of 1,607.4 ha (3,972.0 ac). The mean area was 66.4 ha (164.0 ac) with a 178.3 ha (440.5 ac) standard deviation. Two towns were black-tailed prairie dog towns totaling 71.4 ha (176.4 ac).

The 1980–1989 survey results for the Meeteetse Metapopulation:

There were 49 active white-tailed towns occupying 4,736.7 ha (11,704.6 ac) with a minimum area of 0.04 ha (0.1 ac) and a maximum of 1,607.4 ha (3,972.0 ac). The mean area was 96.7 ha (239.0 ac) with a 242.6 ha (599.5 ac) standard deviation.

The 1980–1989 survey results for the Basin Metapopulation:

There were 56 active white-tailed towns occupying 2,294.7 ha (5,670.3 ac) with a minimum area of 0.008 ha (0.02 ac) and a maximum of 631.4 ha (1,560.1 ac). The mean area was 40.8 ha (100.8 ac) with an 89.9 ha (222.2 ac) standard deviation. Two towns were black-tailed prairie dog towns totaling 71.3 ha (176.4 ac).

The 2001–2005 survey results for the Total Population:

There were 66 active white-tailed towns occupying 2,011.5 ha (4,970.6 ac) with a minimum area of 0.08 ha (0.2 ac) and a maximum of 572.1 ha (1,413.8 ac). The mean area was 29.8 ha (73.7 ac) with a 75.6 ha (186.7 ac) standard deviation. Four towns were black-tailed prairie dog towns totaling 77.4 ha (191.3 ac), an increase of 8 percent.

The 2001–2005 survey results for the Meeteetse Metapopulation:

There were 5 active white-tailed towns occupying 615.2 ha (1,520.1 ac) with a minimum area of 1.0 ha (2.5 ac) and a maximum of 572.1 ha (1,413.8 ac). The mean area was 123.0 ha (304.0 ac) with a 251.3 ha (621.0 ac) standard deviation.

The 2001–2005 survey results for the Basin Metapopulation:

There were 61 active white-tailed towns occupying 1,396.4 ha (3,450.5 ac) with a minimum area of 0.08 ha (0.2 ac) and a maximum of 271.7 ha (671.5 ac). The mean area was 22.7 ha (56.0 ac) with a 38.4 ha (94.9 ac) standard deviation. Four towns were black-tailed prairie dog towns totaling 77.4 ha (191.3 ac).

The mean nearest neighbor distance between white-tailed towns for the 2001–2005 survey was 2,013 m, with a minimum of 60 m, maximum of 9,057 m, and a standard error of 279.7. The mean nearest distance between towns for the 1980–1989 survey was 1,963 m, with a minimum of 48 m, maximum of 13,243 m, and a standard error of 235.7. The white-tailed prairie dog population also comprised 96 percent of the occupied prairie dog area and 4 percent of the area was occupied by black-tailed prairie dogs for the 2001–2005 survey.

The percent decrease in occupied area occurring between the 1980–1989 surveys and the 2001–2005 survey was 71 percent for the Total Population, 87 percent for the Meeteetse Metapopulation, and 39 percent for the Basin Metapopulation (Table 1 and Figure 2). The 2001–2005 Basin Metapopulation and Total Population had a smaller active mean town area than the 1980–1989 Total Population (Table 1). The 2001–2005 Meeteetse Metapopulation mean town area was larger than the 1980–1989 Meeteetse Metapopulation.

Table 1. Attributes of white-tailed prairie dog towns surveyed during 1980–1989 and 2001–2005.

	1980–1989 Survey	2001–2005 Survey	Percent Difference
Total Population			
Town Abundance	105	66	37 percent decrease
Occupied Area	7,031.8 ha (17,374.9 ac)	2,011.5 ha (4,970.6 ac)	71 percent decrease
Mean Town Area	66.4 ha (164.0 ac)	29.8 ha (73.7 ac)	55 percent decrease
Meeteetse Metapopulation			
Town Abundance	49	5	90 percent decrease
Occupied Area	4,736.7 ha (11,704.6 ac)	615.2 ha (1,520.1 ac)	87 percent decrease
Mean Town Area	96.7 ha (239.0 ac)	123.0 ha (304.0 ac)	79 percent increase
Basin Metapopulation			
Town Abundance	56	61	8 percent increase
Occupied Area	2,294.7 ha (5,670.3 ac)	1,396.4 ha (3,450.5 ac)	39 percent decrease
Mean Town Area	40.8 ha (100.8 ac)	22.7 ha (56.0 ac)	44 percent decrease

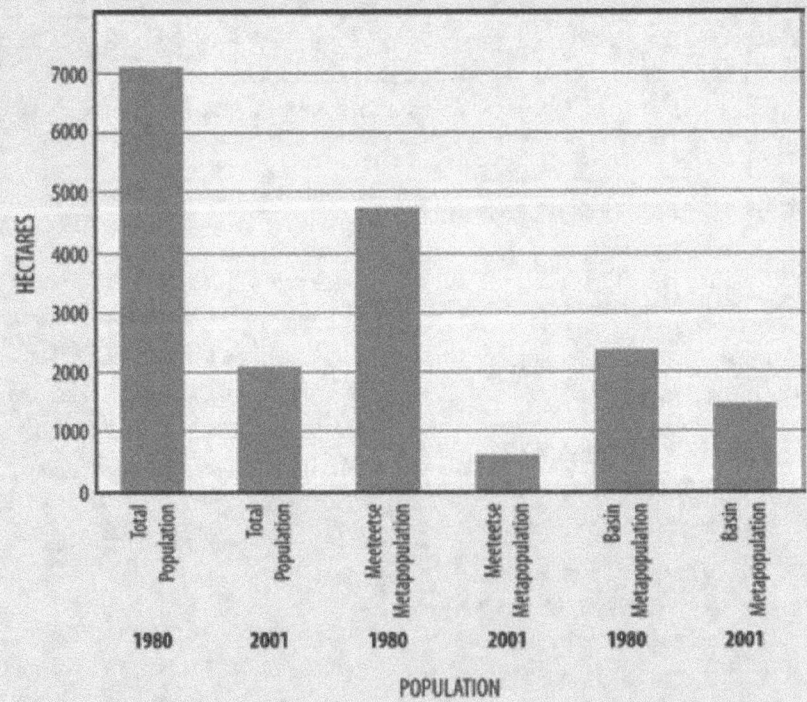

Figure 2. Comparison of hectares occupied by white-tailed prairie dogs for the Total Population, Meeteetse Metapopulation, and Basin Metapopulation during the two surveys beginning in 1980 and 2001.

Burrow density and activity within the Basin Metapopulation appears to have changed over time (Figures 3 and 4; Table 2). There was a trend towards more inactive burrows in both the ≤10 and >10 burrows per 0.405 ha (1.0 ac) categories for the 2001–2005 survey and were significantly associated with the time since the 1980-1989 survey ($X^2 = 12.76$, P < 0.006, Cramer's V = 0.24) (Figures 3 and 4; Table 2).

Table 2. Basin Metapopulation percent change during the time between the two surveys of active and inactive burrows within active white tailed prairie dog towns categorized as ≤ 10 or >10 burrows per 0.405 ha (1.0 ac) categories.

	Active	Inactive
≤10	-32 percent	+100 percent
>10	-33 percent	+71 percent

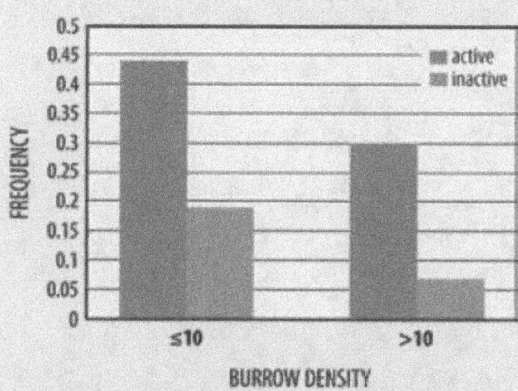

Figure 3. Basin Metapopulation frequency of active and inactive burrow density estimates within active white-tailed prairie dog towns categorized as ≤10 or >10 burrows per 0.405 hectare (1.0 ac) for the 1980–1989 survey.

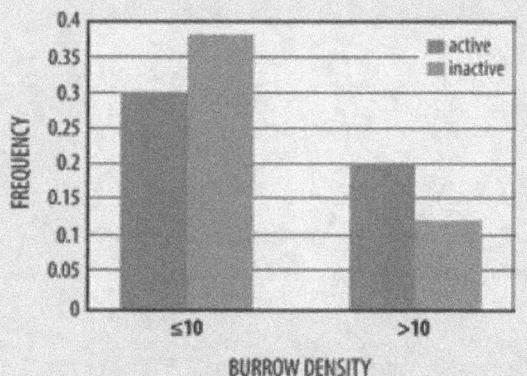

Figure 4. Basin Metapopulation frequency of active and inactive burrow density estimates within active white-tailed prairie dog towns categorized as ≤10 or >10 burrows per 0.405 hectare (1.0 ac) for the 2001–2005 survey.

Habitat Associations

A two-dimensional chi-square test of the five most frequent range sites showed a significant association between the actual range site areas selected by white-tailed prairie dogs when compared to potential dispersal site areas available within the potential dispersal area (2.7 km) ($X^2 = 77.67$, P < 0.0001 and Cramer's V = 0.017) (Figure 5). Of the soil types present in active white-tailed prairie dog towns, saline uplands and loamy sites were often a major soil component and were most frequently used. They made up 32.6 percent and 22.8 percent of the total active white-tailed prairie dog town area respectively (Figure 5).

Saline upland and loamy sites appear to be associated with white-tailed prairie dog distribution, as soils in the potential dispersal area were relatively less frequent (Figure 5). The two largest differences between the actual areas selected and the potential areas available were in clayey and shale range sites. This illustrates a higher frequency of use of these sites than the amount theoretically available to them. Saline uplands and loamy sites were most common; however, white-tailed prairie dogs appear to have a high selective propensity for infrequent clayey and shale range sites. There appears to be some selection for loamy sites; however, for shallow loamy, the actual and potential percent selection was identical (Figure 5).

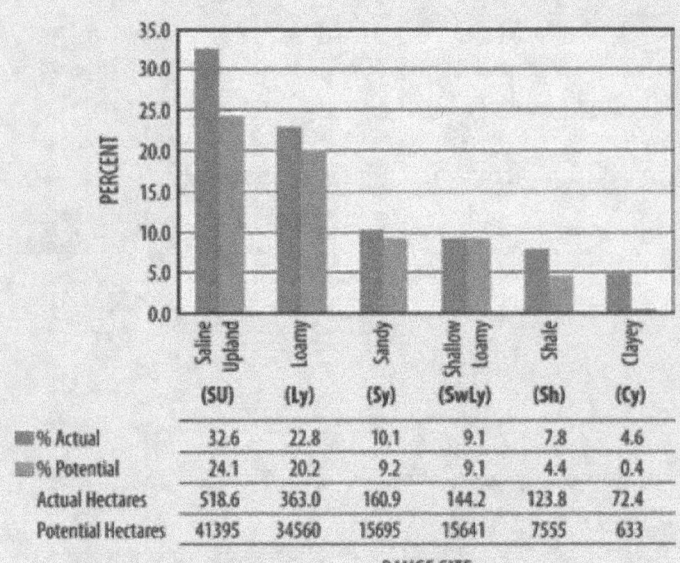

	Saline Upland (SU)	Loamy (Ly)	Sandy (Sy)	Shallow Loamy (SwLy)	Shale (Sh)	Clayey (Cy)
% Actual	32.6	22.8	10.1	9.1	7.8	4.6
% Potential	24.1	20.2	9.2	9.1	4.4	0.4
Actual Hectares	518.6	363.0	160.9	144.2	123.8	72.4
Potential Hectares	41395	34560	15695	15641	7555	633

RANGE SITE

Figure 5. Area and percent of range site area actually occupied by 2001–2005 active white-tailed prairie dog towns compared with potentially occupied areas within 2.7 km.

There also appears to be a significant association between precipitation zones and white-tailed prairie dog distribution ($X^2 = 928.89$, P < 0.0001 and Cramer's V = 0.047). The only zone where the active town occurrence was greater than what was available was in the 20.3–25.4 cm (8–10 in), precipitation zone (Figure 6). Thus, range sites and precipitation zones account for part of the observed variability for site selection. Low Cramer's V values indicate other variables also influence white-tailed prairie dog town site selection.

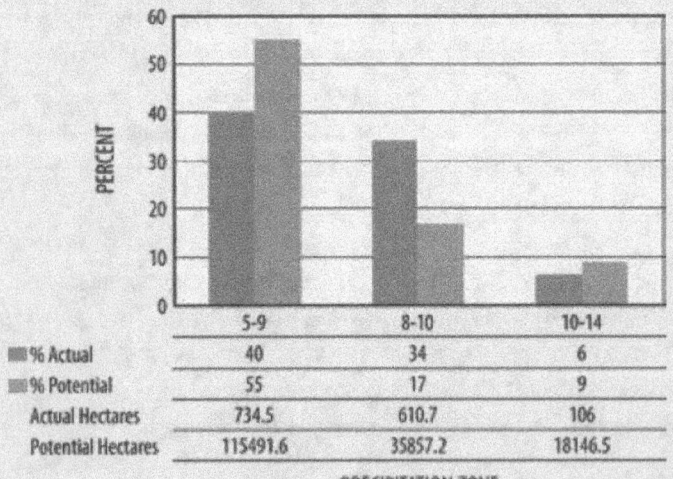

	5-9	8-10	10-14
% Actual	40	34	6
% Potential	55	17	9
Actual Hectares	734.5	610.7	106
Potential Hectares	115491.6	35857.2	18146.5

PRECIPITATION ZONE

Figure 6. Area of land in precipitation zones 12.7–22.9 cm (5–9 in), 20.3–25.4 cm (8–10 in), and 25.4–35.6 cm (10–14 in), occupied by 2001–2005 active white-tailed prairie dog towns and potentially occupied areas within 2.7 km.

Cottontail rabbit occupying an inactive white-tailed prairie dog burrow.

DISCUSSION

THERE APPEARS TO HAVE BEEN MANY CHANGES IN PRAIRIE DOG ACTIVITY and distribution during the relatively short time period (12–26 year range) between the two surveys. Within the study area, black-tailed prairie dog towns appear to have increased slightly, while the Total Population of white-tailed prairie dog towns have decreased as a whole, showing large decreases in four categories: town abundance, occupied area, mean town area, and active burrow density (Tables 1 and 2; Figures 2, 3, and 4). In other words, active white-tailed prairie dog towns were fewer, smaller, and more inactive.

Although the black-tailed prairie dog population increased slightly, it may be vulnerable since they are so rare and isolated from the rest of the species' range. White-tailed prairie dogs are by far the most common prairie dog species in the study area, which is probably due to their adaptations for sagebrush vegetation communities (Hoogland 1996).

The two white-tailed prairie dog meta-populations (Meeteetse Metapopulation and Basin Metapopulation) within the Total Population appear to have changed in different ways. The Meeteetse Meta-population, where black-footed ferrets were found, showed the largest decline. There are fewer, but larger towns, covering much less area (a large decrease in occupied area and town abundance, and an increase in the mean town area - Table 1). This suggests that surviving white-tailed prairie dogs may have contracted to core areas, possibly resulting in part from epizootic and enzootic plague, along with many other cumulative factors (Menkens and Anderson 1991; Cully and Williams 2001). Currently this metapopulation has become much less suitable for black-footed ferrets, although it may rebound to a suitable size where ferrets could one day be returned to where the recovery source population was found.

The Basin Metapopulation appears to have become more fragmented. There are more, but smaller towns, which cover less area (occupied area and mean town area both decreased, while the town abundance increased - Table 1). Within the Basin Metapopulation, white-tailed prairie dogs may be more easily fragmented than the Meeteetse Metapopulation due to highways, urban areas, and other development interspersed throughout the population.

Within the Basin Metapopulation, there was also a significant association between categorical estimates of active and inactive burrow densities between the 1980–1989 BLM surveys and the 2001–2005 survey.

Comparisons of burrow density could not be made in the Meeteetse Metapopulation because data were not collected with the same methods. These results suggest that during the time between the two surveys, there must have been certain factors causing a shift from relatively higher to lower density estimates of active burrows and an increase in inactive burrow density estimates (Figures 3 and 4). Causal factors of this shift and the other observed demographic declines were not analyzed and may be any of the identified causes for declines (Cully and Williams 200; Pauli et al. 2006; Seglund et al. 2004); however, enzootic plague may be a plausible explanation since plague has been detected every year sampled in the Meeteetse Metapopulation by the U.S. Geological Survey from 1988–2008 (Dean Biggins per. comm.).

Trends in these colony attributes are the best available indicators of prairie dog population trends in the northern Bighorn Basin. Thus, considering the overall decrease in occupied area and a proportional shift from more active burrows to more inactive burrows, the white-tailed prairie dog population within this study area appears to have exhibited negative trends in population distribution and abundance (Lomolino and Smith 2001). Efforts to reverse these trends should be implemented before further decreases occur, which could further reduce the overall white-tailed prairie dog range and distribution. Another short-term decline could lead to additional justification for listing under the Endangered Species Act of 1973.

These results should be interpreted cautiously due to potential biases and limitations of the study design. It is quite difficult to accurately and precisely replicate historical surveys where the goal is to inventory prairie dog distribution and activity (Seglund et al. 2004). This study assumes that all towns in the study area were included in this analysis, or at least that the levels of detection were the same for both surveys. The results of both surveys are likely underestimated, biased towards prairie dog towns on Federal and State-administered lands, and larger towns. Because access to private land was not possible in all cases, there may be prairie dog towns that were not detected during the surveys.

In order to compare 12–26 year old survey data to the present survey data, the 1980–1989 surveys methods were replicated and limitations for both surveys were assumed to be similar. Access to land, however, may have changed between the two surveys because of changing land ownership patterns. GPS units were used to map towns, which may have been more accurate than hand-drawn maps from the previous surveys.

Although visual counts might provide more accurate indices to actual populations (Severson and Plumb 1998), the methods used for this study were designed to replicate the former study and time and resources were limited. The results should be appropriate for trend estimates on activity, occupied area, and distribution for the study area (Biggins et al. 1993, 2006; Lomolino and Smith 2001). Attempting to replicate a historical survey by using similar methods has long-term trend analysis value and may be impractical to use more rigorous methods (e.g., visual counts, mark-recapture, and mark-resight on large-scale studies) (Biggins et al. 2006).

Although there are errors with estimating burrow density, the error was reduced by using categories large enough where estimates fall within a low rating of ≤10 or a high rating of >10 inactive or active burrows per 0.405 hectare (1.0 ac). Calibrating observers to estimate high and low burrow densities seems to be a reasonable approach for estimating activity level as categorical frequency data. If there were more resources and time, burrow density transects could have been deployed on every prairie dog town providing for more accurate and precise burrow density and activity data.

The habitat selection phase of this study was aimed at describing the spatial distribution of towns relative to soils, precipitation, and proximity to the nearest town. An area with a perimeter boundary of 2.7 km from all surveyed towns was used for a potential dispersal distance and seems appropriate for comparisons of range site and precipitation zone habitat selection by white-tailed prairie dogs (Clark 1973). The mean minimum distance that was measured between towns (2 km) was less, though similar to observations of Clark (1973) (2.7 km) and Garrett and Franklin (1988) (2.4 km). The mean minimum distance only describes white-tailed prairie dog town spatial distribution, which may be related to many factors including habitat quality, individual dispersal behavior, and habitat fragmentation (Clark 1973; Cambell III and Clark 1981; Coppock and Detling 1986; Weltzin et al. 1997).

Considering the observed declines in this population, minimizing disturbances and managing for possible town expansion within a 2 km buffer zone from prairie dog towns may help maintain current dispersal and prairie dog town connectivity. Buffers around prairie dog towns may need to be adjusted depending upon the disturbance type and local habitat variation. Future surveys could measure the mean minimum distance again and use it as an indicator for how distribution may be trending.

White-tailed prairie dog town sites were significantly associated with certain range sites and precipitation zones. This study's results showed an association with multiple range sites including: saline upland, loamy, shale, and clayey sites. Parker et al. (1975) observed similar sites including dense clay-clayey-saline upland selection. Other variables also likely have an effect on these town locations as the Cramer's V is relatively low (Cramer's V = 0.017).

Other habitat selection variables that may be contributing to declines and distribution may include: range site condition, vegetation and watershed health, soil permeability, and the presence or absence of other wildlife species (Garrett et al. 1982; Ceballos and Reading 1994). Sylvatic plague may be the number one factor, which frequently kills >99 percent of prairie dogs in infected colonies (Cully and Williams 2001). Mortality through shooting or poisoning and habitat loss may also be contributing to the observed declines. All these factors should be studied to explain the cumulative effects contributing to the observed population decline in the northern Bighorn Basin and throughout their range.

This study shows that saline upland, loamy, sandy, shallow loamy, and shale range sites were significantly associated with white-tailed prairie dog town site selection when compared to available habitat within 2.7 km (Figure 5). White-tailed prairie dogs occupied the most area in the 12.7–22.9 cm (5–9 in) precipitation zone and in the saline uplands range site; however, loamy sites and the 20.3–25.4 cm (8–10 in) precipitation zone have the highest proportion of actual

active area than what is proportionally potentially available within the 2.7 km buffer (Figures 5 and 6). This suggests that white-tailed prairie dogs may be more successful within this range site and precipitation zone. Also, available range sites less suitable for white-tailed prairie dog towns, such as rock outcrops and impervious clays, were nearly absent from the actual soils used and could be limiting dispersal and site suitability (Garrett et al. 1982). The range site and precipitation zone analyses should be considered a broad scale assessment from soil survey information, using overlapping precipitation zone categories, and may not reflect unique diversity in local conditions. However, these results may help to refine existing habitat suitability models.

Soil types may also be chosen by white-tailed prairie dogs for their structural components (Flath and Paulick 1979). Many soils could be difficult to tunnel in and inhibit dispersal. A shallow soil may not allow enough depth to bedrock, soils of impervious clays would be very difficult to dig in, being directly in a wetland or floodplain could mean many months of inundation, and sandy soils lacking any other matrix could be prone to collapse (Pauli et al. 2006). Soils with high percentages of clay would lack permeability, which could increase flooding and standing water in burrows. This study's results suggest and it would seem reasonable that a loamy soil would be most suitable, as tunnels may require a proportion of clay to hold the walls, yet the addition of sand and silt would allow for easier burrowing.

Since prairie dogs can have higher survivorship in areas with more vigorous forbs, grasses, and sedges, historically they may have built their towns on more productive

loamy sites, possibly those which are now primarily agricultural tracts (Garrett et al. 1982). It is hard to say how much present land conditions and uses prohibit prairie dogs from expanding their range. However, practices such as grazing and agriculture regularly occur on the most productive soils and have displaced prairie dog towns (Koford 1958). White-tailed prairie dogs currently occupy soils, whose alkalinity, texture, lack of depth, and lower precipitation are not generally converted to agriculture. These less productive sites may not adequately provide all life history requirements and perhaps may be all the suitable land that is left to occupy in a fairly undeveloped or seasonally undisturbed state (Garrett et al. 1982). This survey shows current soil selection and may not represent historical, undisturbed habitat selection. Studies of town locations before settlement would illustrate which range sites were used in a less disturbed ecosystem; however, historical evidence may be uncommon and is likely eroding fast.

Soils and precipitation appear to have an effect on habitat selection by prairie dogs. Displacement from these preferred areas may contribute to the observed decline within the study area. There are surely other habitat and anthropogenic variables influencing the prairie dog decline. Plague epizootics caused by flea-transmitted bacteria and recreational shooting can substantially affect prairie dog town persistence (Lechleitner et al. 1968; Pauli et al. 2006; Pauli and Buskirk 2007) and it is likely that plague has had overwhelming influence on prairie dog population dynamics (Dean Biggins per. comm.). Investigations on how natural habitat selection is influenced by anthropogenic factors should be studied further and may reveal additive effects on normal population fluctuations.

Reversing the observed negative population trend is important for conserving a species that provides a prey base for a complex ecosystem and habitat for species, which are BLM sensitive species or listed under the Endangered Species Act of 1973, such as: black-footed ferret, burrowing owl *(Athene cunicularia)*, mountain plover *(Charadrius montanus)*, and ferruginous hawk *(Buteo regalis)* (Bangert and Slobodchikoff 2000). This is a short and incomplete species list for an ecosystem dependent upon the presence and distribution of prairie dogs (Campbell and Clark 1981; Ceballos and Reading 1994; Miller et al. 1994; Desmond and Savidge 1996; Bangert and Slobodchikoff 2000).

LITERATURE CITED

Bangert, R.K. and C.N. Slobodchikoff. 2000. The Gunnison's prairie dog structures a high desert grassland landscape as a keystone engineer. Journal of Arid Environments 46:357-369.

Biggins, D.E., B.J. Miller, L.R. Hanebury, B. Oakleaf, A.H. Farmer, R. Crete, and A. Dood. 1993. A technique for evaluating black-footed ferret habitat. Proceedings of the Symposium on the Management of Prairie Dog Complexes for the Reintroduction of the Black-footed Ferret. USDI Fish and Wildlife Service. Biological Report 13:73-88.

Biggins, D.E., J.G. Sidle, D.B. Seery, and A.E. Ernst. 2006. Estimating the abundance of prairie dogs. In: Hoogland, J.L., (ed.). Conservation of the black-tailed prairie dog: saving North America's western grasslands. Washington, DC: Island Press. p. 94-107.

Bond, R.M. 1945. Range rodents and plant succession. Trans North American Wildlife Conference 10:229-234.

Campbell III, T.M. and T.W. Clark. 1981. Colony characteristics and vertebrate associates of white-tailed and black-tailed prairie dogs in Wyoming. American Midland Naturalist 105(2):269-276.

Cambell III, T.M., T.W. Clark, L. Richardson, S.C. Forrest, and B.R. Houston. 1987. Food habits of Wyoming black-footed ferrets. American Midland Naturalist 117(1):208-210.

Clark, T.W. 1973. A field study of the ecology and ethology of the white-tailed prairie dog (Cynomys leucurus): with a model of Cynomys evolution. Ph.D. dissertation, University of Wisconsin, Madison.

Clark, T.W. and M.R. Stromberg. 1987. Mammals in Wyoming. University Press of Kansas. Lawrence, Kansas, USA.

Coppock, D.L. and J.K. Detling. 1986. Alteration of bison and black-tailed prairie dog grazing interaction by prescribed burning. Journal of Wildlife Management 50(3):452-455.

Coy, S.G. and D.A. Roberts. 1985. Prairie dog ecosystem habitat management plan. USDI Bureau of Land Management. No. WY-010-WHA-T14.

Cully, J.F. and E.S. Williams. 2001. Inter-specific comparisons of Sylvatic plague in prairie dogs. Journal of Mammalogy 82(4):894-905.

Desmond, M.J. and J.A. Savidge. 1996. Factors influencing burrowing owl (Speotyto cunicularia) nest densities and numbers in western Nebraska. American Midland Naturalist 136(1):143-148.

Flath, D.L. and R.K. Paulick. 1979. Mound characteristics of white-tailed prairie dog maternity burrows. American Midland Naturalist 102(2):395-398.

Garrett, M.G. and W.L. Franklin. 1988. Behavioral ecology of dispersal in the black-tailed prairie dog. Journal of Mammology 69(2):236-250.

Garrett, M.G., J.L. Hoogland, and W.L. Franklin. 1982. Demographic differences between an old and a new colony of black-tailed prairie dogs (Cynomys ludovicianus). American Midland Naturalist 108(1):51-59

Harlow, H.J. and Menkens G.E., Jr. 1986. A comparison of hibernation in the black-tailed prairie dog, white-tailed prairie dog, and Wyoming ground squirrel. Canadian Journal of Zoology/Revue Canadienne de Zoologie 64(3):793-796.

Hillman, C.N., R.L. Linder, and R.B. Dahlgren. 1979. Prairie dog distribution in areas inhabited by black-footed ferrets. American Midland Naturalist 102(1):185-187.

Holland, E.A., and J.K. Detling. 1990. Plant response to herbivory and belowground nitrogen cycling. Ecology 71(3):1040-1049.

Hoogland, J.L. 1996. Cynomys ludovicianus. Mammalian Species 535:1-10.

Hoogland, J.L. 2001. Black-tailed, Gunnison's and Utah prairie dogs reproduce slowly. Journal of Mammalogy 82(4):917-927.

Knowles, C.J., C.J. Stoner, and S. P. Gieb. 1982. Selective use of black-tailed prairie dog towns by mountain plovers. Condor 84:71-74.

Koford, C.B. 1958. Prairie dogs, whitefaces, and blue grama. Wildlife Monographs 3:1-78.

Lechleitner, R.R., L. Kartman, M.I. Goldenberg, and B.W. Hudson. 1968. An epizootic of plague in Gunnison's prairie dogs (Cynomys gunnisoni) in south-central Colorado. Ecology 49(4):734-743.

Lehmer, E.M. and D.E. Biggins. 2005. Variations in torpor patterns of free-ranging black-tailed and Utah prairie dogs across gradients of elevation. Journal of Mammalogy 86:15-21.

Lomolino, M. and G.A. Smith. 2001. Dynamic biogeography of prairie dog (Cynomys ludovicianus) towns near the edge of their range. Journal of Mammalogy 82(4):937-945.

Lowery, R. 2007. Vassarstats: website for statistical computation. http://faculty.vassar.edu/lowry/VassarStats.html (accessed Feb. 25, 2007).

Menkens, G.E., Jr. 1987. Temporal and spatial variation in white-tailed prairie dog (Cynomys leucurus) populations and life histories in Wyoming. Ph.D. dissertation, University of Wyoming, Laramie, USA.

Menkens, G.E., Jr. and S.H. Anderson. 1991. Population dynamics of white-tailed prairie dogs during an epizootic of sylvatic plague. Journal of Mammalogy 72(2):328-331.

Menkens, G.E., Jr. and S.H. Anderson. 1989. Temporal-spatial variation in white-tailed prairie dog demography and life histories in Wyoming. Canadian Journal of Zoology 67:343-349.

Miller, B., G. Ceballos, and R. Reading. 1994. The prairie dog and biotic diversity. Conservation Biology 8(3):677-681.

Osborn, B. and P. Allan. 1949. Vegetation of an abandoned prairie-dog town in tall grass prairie. Ecology 30(3):322-332.

Parker, J.L., G.L. Decker, L. Gray, and O. Muller. 1975. Soil survey of Carbon County area, Montana. U.S. Department of Agriculture, Soil Conservation Service. 137 pp.

Pauli, J.N., S.W. Buskirk, E.S. Williams, and W.H. Edwards. 2006. A plague epizootic in the black-tailed prairie dog (Cynomys ludovicianus). Journal of Wildlife Diseases 42(1):74-80.

Pauli, J.N. and S.W. Buskirk. 2007. Recreational shooting of prairie dogs: a portal for lead entering wildlife food chains. Journal of Wildlife Management 71(1):103-108.

Rosenstock, S.S. and C. Van Riper III. 2001. Breeding bird responses to juniper woodland expansion. Journal of Range Management 54(3):226-232.

Seglund, A.E., A.E. Ernst, M. Grenier, B. Luce, A. Puchniak, and P. Schnurr. 2004. White-tailed prairie dog conservation assessment. Unpublished Report.

Severson, K.E. and G.E. Plumb. 1998. Comparison of methods to estimate population densities of black-tailed prairie dogs. Wildlife Society Bulletin 26(4):859-866.

Tileston, J.V. and R.R. Lechleitner. 1966. Some comparisons of the black-tailed and white-tailed prairie dogs in north-central Colorado. American Midland Naturalist 75(2):292-316.

Weltzin, J.F., S. Archer, and R.K. Heitschmidt. 1997. Small-mammal regulation of vegetation structure in a temperate savanna. Ecology 78(3):751-763.